Q&A Kids

LIGHT

AMY CHAPMAN
ANGELIKA SCUDAMORE

WINDMILL BOOKS

Published in 2026 by Windmill Books,
an Imprint of Rosen Publishing
2544 Clinton St.
Buffalo, NY 14224

First published in Great Britain in 2026
by Wayland

Editor: Sarah Peutrill
Designer: Lisa Peacock

Some of the text in this book was
first published in Fact Cat: Light
by Izzi Howell

Cataloging-in-Publication Data

Names: Chapman, Amy, author. | Scudamore, Angelika, illustrator.
Title: Light / Amy Chapman, illustrated by Angelika Scudamore.
Description: Buffalo, NY : Windmill Books, 2026. | Series: Q & A kids | Includes glossary and index.
Identifiers: ISBN 9781725396227 (pbk.) | ISBN 9781725396234 (library bound) | ISBN 9781725396241 (ebook)
Subjects: LCSH: Light--Juvenile literature.
Classification: LCC QC360.C437 2026 | DDC 535.'4--dc23

Printed in the United States of America

CPSIA Compliance Information: Batch #CSWM26
For Further Information contact Rosen Publishing
at 1-800-237-9932

Find us on

CONTENTS

What Is Light?	4
The Color of Light	6
Natural Sources of Light	8
Human-Made Light	10
Sunlight	12
Light and Materials	14
Shadows	16
Shadows Through the Day	18
Shadow Patterns	20
Seeing Things	22
Close Your Eyes	24
Reflective Surfaces	26
Reflections	28
Quiz and Glossary	30
Index and Some Answers	32

Can you spot the glow worms in this book? There are 14 to find, not counting me.

WHAT IS LIGHT?

Q. What is light?

A. The light that we see is part of the energy that the Sun makes that our eyes can detect.

Light is important to all living things. Without sunlight, there would be no plants, animals, or people on Earth.

We use light in many ways. Electric lights help us to see when it is dark. Television and computer screens light up so you can see them. Traffic lights tell vehicles when to stop or go.

FIND IT

Can you find five things in the picture that are giving off light?

THE COLOR OF LIGHT

Q. Is light yellow or white?

A. Neither! It is really made up of different colors. You can see these when light shines through raindrops and makes a rainbow.

The seven rainbow colors of light are: red, orange, yellow, green, blue, indigo, and violet.

THINK ABOUT IT
What is wrong with the rainbow shown above?

FIND IT
Find something of each color of the rainbow in the fairground picture.

NATURAL SOURCES OF LIGHT

Q. Is the Sun the only source of light?

A. No, there are many sources of light.

Some sources are natural. The Sun is a natural source of light. Other natural sources are lightning and fire.

Lightning is a bright flash of light in the sky during a thunderstorm.

Fireflies are insects that make their own light in their bodies. What type of worm makes its own light?

SPOT IT
How many fireflies can you see in the picture?

HUMAN-MADE LIGHT

Q. Are candles a natural source of light?

A. No, candles are something that people have made themselves to make light. Sources of light that are not natural are called human-made.

Flashlights, lamps, and computer screens are other sources of human-made light.

Fireworks are a human-made light source. Light from fireworks can be many different colors.

THINK ABOUT IT

These children are playing a game to find beanbags with flashlights. Why is it tricky to find them even with the flashlights?

SUNLIGHT

Q. Does light from the Sun reach Earth right away?

A. No, it takes 8 minutes and 20 seconds for light from the Sun to reach Earth. But that is fast! Light is the fastest thing in the universe. It travels at around 186,000 miles (300,000 km) per hour.

The Sun is our biggest source of light. It sends out light in all directions through space. Some light eventually reaches Earth.

Light always travels in straight lines. You can see the lines as the Sun shines through these trees.

Light from the Sun is incredibly bright. It only takes a few seconds for sunlight to harm your eyes. You should never look directly at the Sun.

THINK ABOUT IT

What ways can you think of to protect yourself in the Sun? Look for clues in the picture.

LIGHT AND MATERIALS

Q. What happens when light hits something?

A. Light can either be blocked by a material or it can travel through some materials.

We can see through transparent materials because they let light pass through them.

Translucent materials only let a little light through, so you cannot see through them very clearly.

Plastic can be transparent, translucent, or opaque (say *oh-payk*). You cannot see through opaque materials at all.

FIND IT

What is transparent in this picture? Choose two things that are opaque.

SHADOWS

Q. Why do I cast a shadow?

A. Because you are a solid object that light cannot pass through!

A shadow is a dark shape made when light is blocked by an opaque object. When sunlight hits a tree, a building, or a person, it casts a shadow.

Shadows are the same shape as the object blocking the light. If the object moves, the shadow will also move.

Translucent objects make shadows because they do not let all light through them. Why don't transparent objects make shadows?

MATCH IT

Match the shadows with the children that made them.

SHADOWS THROUGH THE DAY

Q. Why is my shadow sometimes long and sometimes short?

A. Shadows change throughout the day. This is because the size of a shadow depends on where the Sun is in the sky.

The Sun makes long shadows in the morning and short shadows in the middle of the day.

Shadows also change position. If the Sun is behind you, your shadow will be in front of you. If the Sun is in front of you, your shadow will be behind you.

THINK ABOUT IT

Look at the picture to see how shadows change throughout the day. Are shadows long or short in the evening? What happens to your shadow on a dark night?

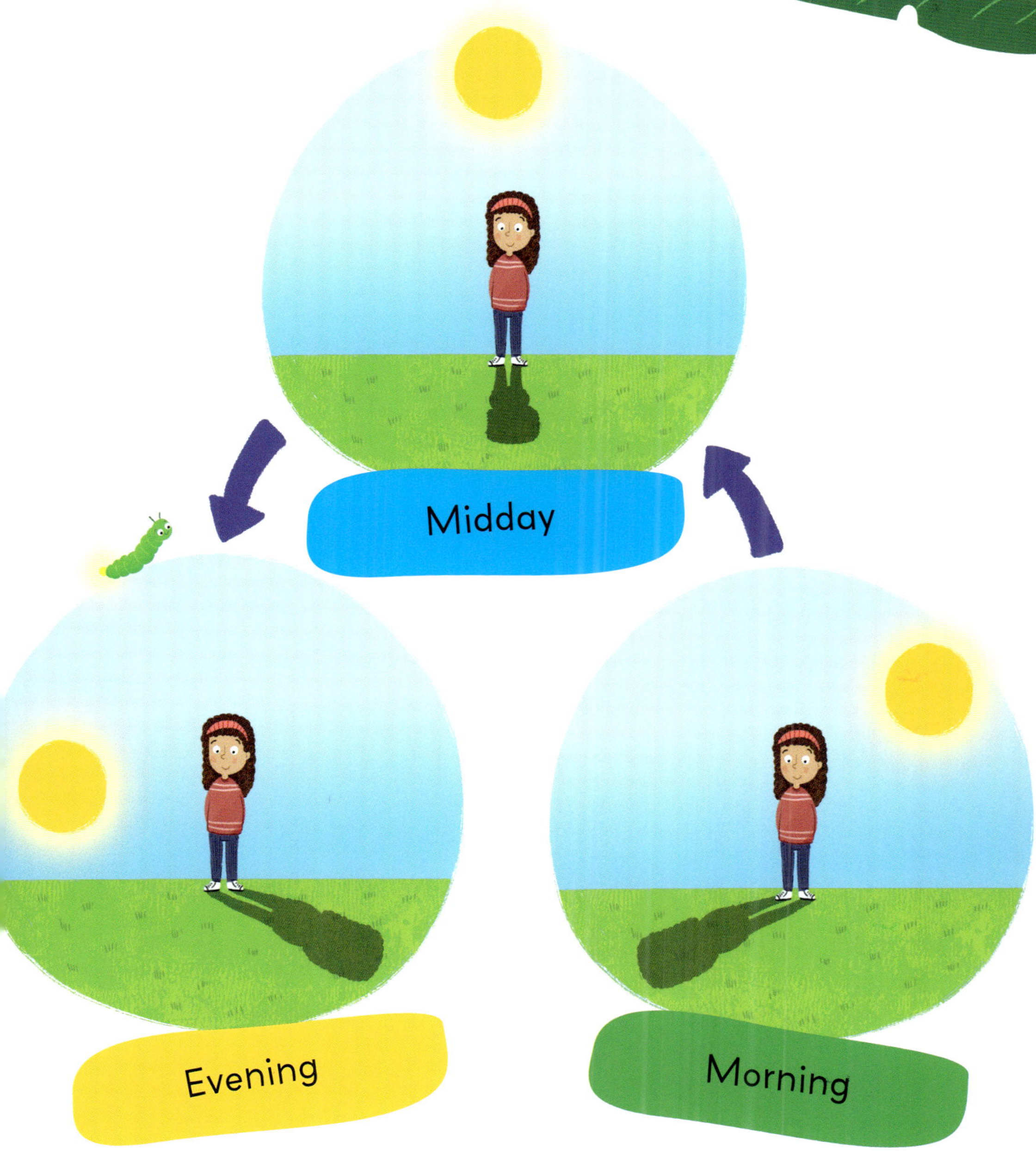
Midday
Evening
Morning

SHADOW PATTERNS

Q. Why is my shadow sometimes bigger?

A. Shadows change the nearer or further the object is from the light source.

If you move an object closer to a light source, its shadow gets bigger. If you move the object further away, it gets smaller.

Stand between a lamp and a white wall. Make shapes with your hands. See how the shadow changes as you move your hands closer to and further away from the lamp.

FIND IT

A flashlight has been moved to different positions to light the toy. Which one shows the flashlight the nearest to the toy and which shows it furthest away?

A.

B.

C.

D.

SEEING THINGS

Q. Why can't I see in the dark?

A. When light hits an object, it reflects (bounces) off it. The reflected light enters your eyes. That is how you see things. It is hard to see things in the dark because no light enters your eyes.

When there is light, it enters your eyes through the pupil (the black part in the middle) of your eyes. When there is less light, your pupils get bigger. This lets more light in to help you see better.

Human-made light sources like flashlights help you see in the dark.

LOOK AT IT

Look at the pupils in the eyes on page 23. Which person is in the darkest room? Which is in the lightest room?

A.

B.

C.

D.

CLOSE YOUR EYES

Q. Why can't I see when I close my eyes?

A. Your eyelids are opaque and when you close them no light can get into your eyes to help you see.

Some people are blind, which means they cannot see well or at all. Some blind people can see some light and can tell when a light is on or off.

Blind people have to use their other senses, such as their hearing, to help them understand the world.

THINK ABOUT IT

Emily and Stella are playing a game. Emily has a blindfold on so she can't see. Stella has to give her instructions to get to the door. moving around the objects. What should she say?

Now you need to move ...

REFLECTIVE SURFACES

Q. The Moon is often bright. Does it make light like the Sun?

A. No, the Moon might look bright, but it does not make its own light. It reflects light from the Sun.

Some objects on Earth reflect light from light sources too. Smooth, shiny surfaces reflect light better than rough, dull surfaces.

Metal and glass are good light reflectors. The glass in buildings sometimes reflects the images of objects and other buildings.

Reflective surfaces are very useful. Car mirrors let drivers see the road behind them. Road reflectors reflect headlights at night to light up the road.

LOOK AT IT

This cyclist is wearing a vest with reflective strips to make sure she can be seen. What other light sources is she using to stay safe?

REFLECTIONS

Q. Why do we see reflections?

A. Reflections are pictures of objects on reflective surfaces. When light bounces off a reflective surface you see a reflection. A reflection is the same as the real object, but it is back to front.

Light bounces evenly off very smooth shiny surfaces, like glass and mirrors. This makes the reflection very clear.

THINK ABOUT IT

This zebra's reflection looks a bit different to the real zebra. Why do you think that is?

QUIZ

1. Which of these is a natural light source?
a) traffic lights
b) a street lamp
c) a star

2. How long does it take sunlight to reach Earth?
a) about 8 minutes
b) about 8 hours
c) about 8 days

3. Transparent materials do not let any light through. True or not true?
a) true
b) not true

4. What happens to a shadow when you move a light source nearer to an object?
a) it gets bigger
b) it gets smaller
c) it stays the same size

5. The Moon does not make its own light. True or not true?
a) true
b) not true

6. Which surface reflects light best?
a) a swimming pool
b) a mirror
c) a cardboard box

Quiz answers
1. c – a star
2. a – about 8 minutes
3. b – not true
4. a – it gets bigger
5. a – true, it reflects sunlight
6. b – a mirror

GLOSSARY

directions the paths that things move along or the places they point to

human-made describes things that are made by people

light sources things that give out light

lightning flashes of light in the sky during a thunderstorm

materials the substances that objects are made of

metal a hard, shiny substance

mirrors smooth, shiny objects that reflect light well

natural describes things that are found in nature, which are not made by people

opaque describes something that does not let any light through

pupils the black openings in the center of your eyes that let in light

reflect when light bounces off an object

reflection the picture formed when light bounces off a smooth surface

screens the front part of televisions and computers

shadow a dark shape created when light is blocked by an object

sunlight the light that comes from the Sun

surface the outside layer of something

translucent describes something that lets a bit of light through but not all of it

transparent describes something that lets all light through

INDEX

blind 24

colors 6, 10

eyes 4, 12, 22, 24, 26

fireflies 8

lightning 8

Moon 26

opaque materials 14, 16, 24

pupils (of eyes) 22

rainbows 6
reflected light 22, 26, 28
reflections 28

shadows 16–21
sources of light 8, 10
  human-made 10
  natural sources 8

Sun 4, 8, 12–13, 18, 26
sunlight 4, 12–13, 16

translucent materials 14, 17
transparent materials 14, 17

SOME ANSWERS

p. 4 glow worm; lamp; streetlight; car headlamp, mobile phone screen
p. 6 the rainbow colors are in the wrong order
p. 8 there are 22 fireflies
p. 10 the flashlights only give out a beam of light so the children have to hold the flashlights directly over the beanbags to spot them
p. 13 sunglasses; sunhat; sunscreen; long-sleeved shirt; water
p. 14 the greenhouse glass is transparent; many things are opaque including plant pots, leaves, watering can, clothes, the human body
p. 17 A2; B1; C3; D4
p. 18 shadows are long in the evening; you don't have a shadow on a dark night because there is no light
p. 20 A. shows it nearest; D. shows it furthest away
p. 22 A. (darkest room) and D. (lightest room)
p. 24 roughly, it would be: turn left for 2 paces; turn right for 2 paces; turn left for 2 paces; turn left for 2 paces; turn right for 2 paces
p. 27 bike light; helmet light
p. 28 the zebra's reflection is back to front in the water and the water isn't completely still